When Kids Grow Up

Mom's Life
Can Be Better Than Ever

Artemis Rose

For the sacred
relationship beyond
motherhood.

When a mom's kids grow up and
move out,
many moms think:

"Now my best years are behind me."

That is not true.

This time can actually be the most
powerful and happiest time of her
whole life.

Why?
Because now she has:
◦ More time
◦ More freedom
◦ More wisdom
◦ A big heart full of love
◦ A mind that understands how life
really works
That makes her very special.

Big Idea #1:
Mom Gets to Become
Herself Again

When kids are little, moms give a lot of
their energy away.

Now she has all of her energy and
time for herself and her goals.

Now the question becomes:

Who do I want to be now?

Not who she has to be.
Not who others expect.
But who she chooses to be.
The happiest and most successful
moms say:
Now I will grow into my best self.

Big Idea #2:
Meaning Comes
From Three Simple Things

1. *What Do I Believe Is Important?*

A mom should decide:

- What does 'a good life' mean to me?
- What really matters?
- How should people treat each other?
- What kind of person do I want to be?

This is like making her own life rulebook.

2. *What Part of Me Never Got to Come Out?*

Many moms once dreamed of:

- Teaching
- Writing
- Helping people
- Leading
- Creating something beautiful

Those dreams are still alive.

They were just waiting for her permission to show themselves.

Now is the time to bring them to life.

3. *Who Can I Help With What I Know?*

A mom has learned so much from living.

She can:

- Guide younger people
- Teach what she knows
- Be a calm, wise voice
- Make other lives better

That gives life a deep, happy feeling.

Big Idea #3:
Build Something Big and Meaningful

Instead of just staying busy, the happiest moms build one big thing that matters to them.

It could be:

- A book
- A class
- A group
- A project
- A way of helping others

Something she can work on for many years.

This gives her days a purpose.

Big Idea #4:
Taking Care of Her Body and Mind

To enjoy life, a mom must feel strong.

That means:

- Moving her body
- Eating food that helps her think clearly
- Sleeping well
- Spending quiet time alone sometimes

Her body is her tool for living well.

Big Idea #5:
Be a Happy Example
for Her Kids

Now mom's job is not to fix everything.

Her new job is to:

- Live a full life
- Keep learning
- Keep growing
- Show that life gets better with age

When kids see this, they feel safer and prouder.

One Important Truth

Not everyone will understand this path.

Some people stop growing.

Some people get smaller.

Some people are afraid to try new things.

That's okay.

The best lives are built by people brave
enough to grow anyway.

The Biggest Lesson of All

A mom is not meant to disappear when
her kids grow up.

She is meant to become:

- Wiser
- Braver
- Stronger
- Happier
- More herself than ever before

She raised her children.
Now she gets to *raise her self* and *her life*.

Ready for the next phase?

Let's begin.

TO ALL MOTHERS

YOU

ARE

THE

BEST

THING

THAT EVER

HAPPENED TO

THIS WORLD!